The Crisis in Economics and the Hong Kong Response

Hong Kong Institute of Economic Science

VICTORIA PRESS

**37782 Los Arboles Drive
Fremont, CA 94536**

The Crisis in Economics and the Hong Kong Response

First published 1984

ISBN 0-9613204-1-9

Printed in Hong Kong

Contents

Contents

Part One

The Crisis in Economics: The Need for New Methodology and First Principles

Economics is a science of thinking in terms of models joined to the art of choosing models which are relevant to the contemporary world. ...Good economists are scarce because the gift for using "vigilant observation" to choose good models, although it does not require a highly specialized intellectual technique, appears to be a very rare one.

J. M. Keynes
Collected Works, Volume IV

The Crisis

That economics is in a state of crisis has been commonly recognized for many years. But what is needed to lead economics out of this crisis has not yet emerged. Within the profession, there is no lack of intellectual ferment and enquiries into the nature and the roots of the crisis. But to this date, no major breakthrough appears to have dawned. Such a state is to be expected, for as long as the true nature of the crisis has not been fully understood, there is no clear direction as to which way a new economics is to be built.

Historically, there has always been a lot of concern over the limitations of orthodox economics. But it was the general disillusionment with the Keynesian orthodoxy and the "grand neoclassical synthesis," following the period of stagflation in the 1970s, that triggered the widespread questioning of the theoretical foundations of economics. Not only has the more recently established Keynesian wisdom been called into question, but the long-established tenets of economics have also been challenged. Key concepts such as equilibrium are denounced, definitions of rationality and optimization are criticized, the relation between micro- and macro-economic theory is questioned, etc. In spite of the controversies generated, no consensus has been reached as to the nature of the crisis.

Naturally, competing schools of economic thought today have given divergent interpretations of the crisis depending on what omissions or errors in the orthodoxy that can be compensated for by the particular strength of each of the schools. "Fundamentalists" blame the stagflation of the 1970s on the distorted reading of Keynes and recommend closer study of the Master. Supply-siders point out the ultimate futility and harmful effect of demand management. Monetarists believe that the economic malaises that plague us today stem from too rapid a rate of growth of money supply. To the rational expectationists, the Keynesian method and theory are full of irreparable errors and all existing macroeconomic models are useless for policy evaluation. The neo-Austrian School points out that the crisis arises because the neoclassical orthodoxy fails to recognize the vital functions of the market, such as error correction, expectation formation, effort coordination, etc. To radical economists, orthodox economics is a part of the bourgeoisie ideology and its failure to explain "doomsday capitalism" is but natural. To liberal economists like Galbraith, orthodox economics fails because it has barred political concepts from economic analysis. In his recent comprehensive survey of the state of economics, Lester Thurow points out that the emergence of the crisis reflects the open bankruptcy of the price auction model, regardless of which particular form this model assumes.[1]

Orthodoxy Accused of being Unreal

In spite of the diversity of criticisms against the orthodoxy, one common denominator can be extracted. Orthodox economics, being founded upon unreal assumptions, is incapable of formulating economic reality. But the puzzle for an observer of the contemporary development in economics is that the backbone of this allegedly unreal orthodox economics is not short of defenders. This is most notable in micro-economic equilibrium analysis.[2] If this unshaken practice of equilibrium analysis — involving *inter alia* continued investment of efforts into its study — were not all a matter of mass delusion among academics on the one hand, and, if equilibrium analysis cannot answer the problems posed by its critics on the other, perhaps there is

---

[1] Lester C. Thurow, *Dangerous Currents — the State of Economics* (New York: Random House,1983).

[2] For example, Frank Hahn and Kenneth Arrow argued that while general equilibrium theories may not have anything to tell us about real economies, they remain a serious and valuable part of economics. See Kenneth Arrow and Frank Hahn, *General Competitive Analysis* (San Francisco: Holden Day, 1971), pp. vi-viii. Hahn also said in his presidential address to the Econometrica Society, "The study of equilibria alone is of no help in positive economic analysis; yet it is no exaggeration to say that the technically best work in the last twenty years has been precisely that. It is good to have it, but perhaps the time has now come to see whether it can serve in an analysis of how economies behave." *Econometrica*, 38 (January 1970).

something valid about equilibrium analysis which its apologists have so far failed to point out. Apologists might claim that, though equilibrium theory is unreal, it is nonetheless indispensable for "mirroring reality." While one may accept this as a metaphor alluding to some valid elements in equilibrium analysis, the mirroring reality argument, *qua* argument, is hardly convincing. It is, obviously, difficult to defend how and why something which is admittedly unreal could mirror reality when the appropriate formulation of reality has yet to be constructed. Also unexplained is the question of why efforts should be spent on mirroring reality instead of constructing theories more directly descriptive of reality.

On the other hand, the critics do not seem to be able to advance further than to point out aspects of the economic reality not captured by equilibrium analysis. They have yet to offer a competing foundation for economics of an equal, if not wider scope, which would be sufficient to supplant equilibrium analysis.

As critics rightly point out, equilibrium analysis explicitly or implicitly starts with unrealistic assumptions such as complete knowledge of alternatives among market participants, zero production time, perfect substitutability of production factors and commodities, perfect competition, infinite divisibility of commodities, the existence of a complete set of commodity future markets on which present commodities (or titles to future commodities) can be freely exchanged for titles to future commodities of every kind and date, etc.[3] Since economic reality would never be able to reach these extremities, deductions from such assumptions remain not descriptive of our economic reality.

---

[3]   See E. Malinvaud, *Lectures on Micro-economic Theory*, A. Silvey, tr. (Amsterdam: North-Holland, 1972); see also T. C. Koopmans, "Allocation of Resources and the Price System," in *Three Essays on the State of Economic Science* (New York: McGraw-Hill, 1957),pp.105-26.

But it would be naive to dismiss equilibrium analysis simply because its initial assumptions are not descriptive of any "actualized states" of our economy. Such extremity assumptions, while unattainable in reality, are nevertheless not entirely devoid of content. Market participants do prefer to be as knowledgeable of the market as possible, within the limits of the time and money they can afford to obtain their information. They do prefer to reduce production time so that the uncertainties entailed in planning ahead can be minimized. Substitutability, too, is desired by market participants. Suppliers of commodities certainly do always desire that their customers would accept substitutes they provide and that they have the ability to provide a wider range of commodities within the limits of their capital outlay and know-how. Customers certainly welcome substitutability as protection against dependence on their suppliers.

Part of the significance of these points has already been appreciated by the Austrian School which interprets equilibrium conditions as states giving the direction towards which a free market would approach, but would never be able to reach.[4] But this view is a mere interpretation without a set of theories explaining why, how, and by what mechanisms the actual economy approaches these conditions. Stopping at such an interpretation of equilibrium theory leaves unresolved the paradox that, on the one hand, there does appear to be something real to the allegedly unreal equilibrium theory, but on the other hand, critics of equilibrium theory being unreal has not been able to supply a "real" economics.

---

[4]   Friedrich A. Von Hayek, *Individualism and Economic Order* (Chicago: University of Chicago Press, 1948).

"Theoretical Limits" Versus "Generative Principles"

Our solution to the above paradox is that what is real in equilibrium analysis is that it provides formulations of the different aspects of the "theoretical limits" of the decentralized economic system, in particular the limits of allocative efficiency.[5] Such formulations are either more rigorous versions of the same mode of representation,[6] or they are pursuits towards different systems of representing the limits,[7] or they are made to take into account specialized assumptions, such as money, time, uncertainty, expectation, etc.[8] There is a need to study such limits for, though unactualizable in practice and hence we term them theoretical, they nevertheless are part of reality because they represent the extreme boundaries where reality can reach in principle but cannot go beyond.

Theoretical limits represent the barest essential framework within the boundaries of which other factors — economic or extra-economic — operate, interplay and give rise to economic phenomena. The function of theoretical limits

---

[5]   The equilibrium allocation can be shown to reach the state of Pareto-efficiency.

[6]   For example, Arrow and Debreu established the competitive equilibrium as an analogue of the Nash-equilibrium for an n-person game. Lionel W. McKenzie used the Kakutani fixed-point theorem. David Gale used the Brouwer fixed-point theorem which is a less general one.

[7]   For example, general equilibrium analysis has been rewritten from a game-theoretic perspective over the last two decades. Both Leontiff's input-output model and Sraffa's theory can be looked upon as different approaches of theorizing such limits.

[8]   See Oskar Lange, *Price Flexibility and Employment* (Bloomington, Ind: Principia, 1944).See also Roy Radner, "Competitive Equilibrium Under Uncertainty," *Econometrica* (1968), 31-58, and "Problems in the Theory of Markets Under Uncertainty," *American Economic Review* (May 1970), 458-59.

can be likened to, say, the pillars and beams of a house or the solid container of liquids. Knowledge of beams and pillars which form the structure of a house tells little about its appearance. But it does give useful information about its maximal internal space, the degree to which walls and internal fittings can be altered, etc. Similarly, a container itself tells nothing about the content. But knowledge of the container can tell us about the limits of what can be contained therein, the maximal volume, the maximal resistance to corrosion, the minimal size of its molecule without causing leakage from the container, etc.

With the help of the above analogies, we are in a position to stipulate that theoretical limits are the barest essential framework pertaining to economic entities and processes which render them economic rather than psychological, sociological etc. As frameworks, they are not all that there is to economic reality. They can only give broad shapes to economic phenomena. As can be expected, knowledge of frameworks alone cannot adequately explain economic phenomena. To seek adequate explanation, we would have to include important but less primary economic factors, extra-economic factors which are capable of affecting economic results and, most importantly, the ways in which these factors interact with one another. Nonetheless, knowledge of theoretical limits does provide the indispensable bearing to understanding the significance of other factors as a whole.

We come to recognition of these theoretical limits by two routes. First, some barest minimal essential features can be abstracted about economic entities and processes *qua* such entities and processes. We can then deduce the properties of these barest essentials as a systematic whole. Secondly, we can indirectly test the existence of these limits by deducing what undesirable economic consequences would result if we act wittingly or unwittingly on assumptions contrary

to them. To use an illustrative analogy, we test the limits of
reality by bumping our heads against the wall like Dr.
Johnson did to refute Bishop Berkeley by kicking a stone.

In contrast to theoretical limits are the various "actualized states" of the economy and the underlying "generative principles" responsible for these states. These states, either in their entirety or in part, are what we directly observe or experience in our economic life or through statistics about the directly observable magnitudes of various economic parameters. It is these actualized states and their purported underlying generative principles which we would intuitively regard as the economic reality.

To recapitulate, we have advanced a diacritical analysis of
the economic reality into theoretical limits versus actualized
states to explain to what extent equilibrium analysis is
justifiable and valid and, to what extent criticisms of equilibrium analysis as unreal represent sound judgment on the
crude intuitive level. That part of the economic reality we
have just termed theoretical limits — and to which we have
ascribed to be the subject of equilibrium analysis — is
neither the directly observable part of the economy nor the
generative principles responsible for these observables.
However, it constitutes the minimal essential structure
within which multifarious factors interact to give rise to the
observables.

The concern of orthodox economists with theoretical limits
has one lethal consequence for the development of
economic thought, namely, a vital area of economic reality
other than theoretical limits has been belittled if not
ignored.[9] This is the area of the range and varieties as well

---

[9]   The position, for instance, is lamented by R. M. Cyert and C. L. Hedrick,
     "Theory of the firms: past, present and future," *Journal of Economic
     Literature*, 10 (June 1972), 398-412.

as the patterns of changes among the actualized states of the economy. Even the most detailed and correct account of such theoretical limits does not tell much about the generative principles, that is, principles about the systematic interaction of actions and processes of less-than-perfect agents, and how they move within or approach such limits individually or collectively. Being theories about the limits of reality rather than about the changing real world, it would be wrong to expect equilibrium theory to make the kind of assertion that, if we want to explain such and such economic phenomena, we can point out such and such as underlying factors responsible for them.

It is the area of the actualized states of the economy and the underlying generative principles leading to these states that the layman would regard as real. As the equilibrium theory of orthodox economics is about something else, it follows that critics have accused orthodox economics of being unreal and that such accusation sounds convincing.

If our diacritical analysis of efficiency limits versus generative principles were correct, then, another aspect of the present crisis in economics can also be explained, namely, why it has so far been futile to find a micro foundation for macro-economics from the existing orthodox framework. The reason is that existing orthodox micro-economics, being concerned chiefly with the formulation of theoretical limits, is about a different part of the economic reality other than the subject matters of macro-economics, which being various actualized states, are the results of generative principles in action. In other words, if a formulation could be built to explain macro-economic phenomena, this formulation would have to rest upon theories about generative principles, which are grossly lacking in the orthodox micro-economic framework.

The Drift of Economics Towards the Study of Theoretical Limits

To the student of the history of economic thought, the most bewildering phenomenon is that mainstream economics after Adam Smith confines itself largely to the studies of theoretical limits. Adam Smith, the father of economics, with his theory of the invisible hand, etc., has never lost sight of the operation of generative principles. The set of generative principles expounded by Adam Smith is of course not encompassing enough. But then, at the early stage of the science, less was expected of economics. As more and more was expected of economics, the unfortunate development was that growth in economics was by and large taken up by the more sophisticated studies of theoretical limits rather than by expanding the repertoire of theories about generative principles.

Indeed, the quest for refinement in formulation has unwittingly resulted in preoccupation with studying efficiency limits to the exclusion of studying generative principles.[10] This accounts for the development in economics of many original conceptions that have become sterilized and divorced from reality. Thus competition in the free market has become the impossible state of perfect competition. It has become the impossible state of "economic equalitarianism" whereby abnormal profit is eliminated. The economic man who serves his enlightened self-interest

---

[10] This unending quest for refinement is not necessarily a value in itself, as Karl R. Popper pointed out, "I do not believe that exactness or precision are intellectual values in themselves; on the contrary, we should never try to be more exact or precise than the problem before us requires." See Karl R. Popper, *Objective Knowledge: An Evolutionary Approach*, Revised Edition, (Oxford: Clarendon Press, 1979), p.58. Also,it is pointed out by Kenneth E. Boulding, "The whole profession, indeed, is an example of that monumental misallocation of intellectual resources which is one of the most striking phenomena of our times." See Kenneth Boulding, "The Economics of Knowledge and the Knowledge of Economics," *The American Economic Review*, LVI, No. 2 (1966), 1-13.

has become an "economic god" with omnipotent knowledge. Enlightened self-interest has become the uncom-
promising maximization principle. The economic order,
which is unwittingly produced by the unintended consequences of individuals acting out of self-interest, and which
has the effect of upgrading the well-being of the majority,
has become the instantiation of the impossible state of
equilibrium.

Methodological Extremitism

What has not been fully realized by both the critics and the
practitioners of orthodox micro-economics is that the narrow scope of mainstream micro-economics is dictated by
the very methodology it has been employing in the studying of theoretical limits. Methodologically, it is necessary to
postulate extremities for some of its dominant initial stipulations. By the logic of the axiomatic system, the nature and
shape of the theoretical limits of an economic system can
be deduced only from such extremities.

It is the ideal of any axiomatic system that we start with
minimal assumptions and premises and then try to deduce
the most powerful of conclusions from them.[11] In the search
for the most rigorous minimal starting premises and
assumptions, it is only natural that economics starts with
postulates of extremities. These extremities are among the
barest essentials of economic situations and processes *qua*
such situations and processes. Social, psychological, cultural
factors, etc. that could influence results we regard as
economic are *a fortiori* excluded. This approach is defensi-
ble as a first step to build any science. Such postulates of
extremities, uncomplicated by detracting factors, are amenable to formulation by mathematical tools. Only such formulations can put economics in the favorable light of

---

[11]   J. Bronowski, *A Sense of the Future* (Cambridge: The MIT Press, 1977),
       p.59.

approaching the ideal of the axiomatic method. Otherwise, there does not seem to be any other standard of excellence to justify it. It is therefore understandable that economists have collectively been concentrating on building up a core of economic knowledge on the basis of such methodological tools.

But such borrowing from the ideal of the axiomatic method has exacted a heavy price on economics. Mathematics has adopted the axiomatic method with great success because we do not expect mathematics to be theories about reality.[12] We develop a mathematical system first and apply it to whatever part of reality that the system fits. When the system is not applicable to a certain part of reality, we never consider it to be the shortcoming of mathematics nor our lack of understanding of reality. We just take it that there is insufficient analogue relations between the basic postulates of that branch of mathematics and that part of reality to which we apply the mathematics. For example, our system of positive integers says nothing about reality. We apply them to count discrete objects that stay discrete before and after the counting. When we deal with drops of water that do not stay discrete when put in juxtaposition with one another, we no longer use positive integers to add or subtract the total drops of water.

But we expect more out of the results of equilibrium analysis. We expect equilibrium analysis to serve as the core of economics which can explain the economic reality. But the economic reality is full of results which could be affected by cultural, psychological, political, social factors, etc. One classic example is the study of the protestant ethic

---

[12] Only the ancient mystics regard mathematics as revealing the secrets of the universe. Modern philosophers of mathematics, notably Bertrand Russell, expounded that mathematics is a science in which we do not know what we are talking about. In non-technical terms, this means the field of application is not yet determined when we built a mathematical system.

and the rise of capitalism.[13] As can be expected, equilibrium analysis has no place for such factors. To suit the ideal of the axiomatic method, it has unwittingly and inevitably trimmed the content of its starting premises to the minimal. **In other words, while we expect more out of equilibrium analysis than we have out of mathematics, we have injected as little into the foundation of equilibrium analysis as we have done for any mathematics which says nothing about reality. It is this borrowing from the method and ideal of the axiomatic system coupled with the expectation that the results of equilibrium analysis (and other branches of economics built in the same manner) can fully explain the economic reality, that we term "methodological extremitism."**

We need to further qualify that the use of the axiomatic method — or any method modelled upon it — need not be limited to systems which say nothing about the real world, among which mathematical systems are the most prominent examples. The axiomatic method could nonetheless be extended to study the real world provided we accept some heavy limitations and provided we reduce our aims.[14] The axiomatic method is admirably suited to the study of theoretical limits provided that economists have the skill to abstract some sharply defined aspects of the underlying economic reality from which we can deduce some patterns and shape about that reality. We also have to require of these abstractions that they parallel closely to the causal sequences of reality. And we have also to accept that the patterns and shape of reality so derived are not all that there is to the patterns and regularities to the economic reality. In other words, we just cannot expect of the derivatives from these abstractions to capture a large number of

---

[13] Max Weber, *The Protestant Ethic & the Spirit of Capitalism*, Talcott Parsons, tr. (New York: Charles Scribner's Sons, 1976).

[14] Bronowski, *op.cit.*, p.60.

significant patterns and regularities. Alternatively put, we cannot expect orthodox micro-economics modelled upon the axiomatic method to throw light on the wider part of the economic reality beyond the theoretical limits.

Futility of the Relaxation Approach in Studying Reality[15]

One of the cardinal limitations of methodological extremitism is that relaxation of its initial postulates of extremities cannot bring about a valid way of studying that wider part of economic reality below theoretical limits, as is sometimes believed to be.[16]

The relaxation of any extremity such as perfect knowledge, maximization, etc. is critical enough to significantly weaken the content of that particular economic theory relative to the original theory about theoretical limits.[17] The economic reality as seen through such theories would be amorphous and much less contentful than the original theories about theoretical limits. As a result, such relaxed theories would be even worse than pure theories about theoretical limits. They are neither

---

[15] "Reality" in our broad sense consists of both the tangible real world phenomena as well as the intangible theoretical limits. When this special meaning is used, it will be explicitly mentioned. Otherwise, we follow the conventional meaning of reality to refer to real world phenomena.

[16] For example, Daniel M. Hausman pointed out, "By progressively weakening and complicating the stipulations needed in order to demonstrate the existence of more complex equilibria, we come closer to being able to apply the theory to real economies." See "Are General Equilibrium Theories Explanatory?" *Philosophy in Economics*, J.C. Pitt, ed. (D. Reidel Publishing Company, 1981), p.28.

[17] Indeed, Nicholas Kaldor pointed out, "In fact, these props are never removed; the removal of any one or a number of them — as for example, allowing for increasing returns or learning by doing — is sufficient to cause the whole structure to collapse like a pack of cards." See T. W. Hutchison, *Knowledge & Ignorance in Economics* (Oxford: Basil Blackwell, 1977), p.76.

applicable to the study of theoretical limits nor to the study of reality. In other words, while theories of limits are applicable to a highly restricted part of the economic reality, such "relaxed" extremity theories are applicable to no part of the economic reality at all. Therefore, to defend microeconomic theories in terms of their claim that "relaxed versions" can hopefully be built some day turns out in effect to be valid charges by the critics that orthodox economics is unreal.

Provided that we are aware of the limited scope of the study of orthodox micro-economics, such economics does offer solid contributions to our stock of economic knowledge, no matter how restricted such contributions may be. Ignorance of this vital fact will lead inevitably to false claims and false expectations. The relaxation approach mentioned above represents one of such false expectations. Another consequence of such ignorance is that extremity postulates are used as a starting point for the formulating of related theories intended to study the real world. As can be expected, theories thus generated would not be applicable to any part of reality at all.

The Proper Method to study Economic Reality — "Methodological Gradationism"

The inefficaciousness of methodological extremitism and the impotence of the derivative "relaxation" approach in gaining access to the real world points to the need for an alternative. As relaxed extremity postulates are sterile, we need more pregnant conceptions about the various states of less-than-perfect knowledge, less-than-perfect competition, etc. These more pregnant conceptions would, conversely, be the distinguishing feature setting the theories embodying them categorically apart from other theories about theoretical limits and from those altogether alienated from any part of reality at all.

These conceptions, to be qualitatively distinct from the empty ones of the "relaxation" approach, would have to single out for abstraction those factors or mechanisms by which the economy approaches step by step towards an extremity or departs away from it. With this kind of abstraction, one gets qualitative information about how the economy operates in less-than-perfect states and how the economy moves or drifts away from the extremities. Such theories, if correct, tell us not only how an economy is operating, but also the direction in which its driving forces tend.

As the social and economic reality is manifestedly the very opposite of being monolithic, there are naturally more than one factor or mechanism operating in an economy with reference to any extremity. The right combination of these factor would, therefore, upgrade or downgrade an economic process, or the economy as a whole, to the point next to an extremity or its opposite. A multitude of these factors pertinent to a particular extremity would then constitute a "continuum" of states approaching an extremity or its opposite. Let us call each qualitatively distinct part of this continuum a "gradation." An economic theory or concept would then be able to study the real world if it can either characterize a gradation or be open to incorporation into a gradation.

The requirement that economic theories and concepts purporting to study the real world be related to a gradation can be termed "methodological gradationism" in contradistinction to "methodological extremitism" under which theories about extremities are developed. To further elucidate the nature of a gradation, it would be useful to examine what would not constitute a gradation. To contrast a gradation with a mere taxonomy of extremities, we can take the example of a sheer juxtaposing of a theory of perfect competition with a theory about its opposite, monopoly, together with a theory about a supposedly in between state of oligopoly. The end result of such a jux- taposing would not be a gradation because it would not give us theories about the generative principles whereby an economy or a certain trade moves towards perfect competi- tion or away from it towards oligopoly or monopoly. From this perspective, orthodox treatment of monopoly, oligopoly, etc., would be mere studies of limits albeit of different kinds, rather than gradations — towards or away from perfect competition.

Where Gradationism and Extremitism Yield Similar Results

To recapitulate, we have bifurcated the economic reality into theoretical limits on the one hand and actualized states governed by generative principles on the other. Theories developed under orthodox micro-economics — notably general equilibrium analysis — are suited to the study of theoretical limits while theories developed under methodological gradationism are indispensable for the study of the other wider part of reality consisting of the actualized states and their underlying generative principles.

This parallel between bifurcation of reality *vis-a-vis* bifurcation of methodology is however not a rigid one. There are special cases in which the reality could be studied by both methods and would yield very similar results, that is, in those cases where reality is rather uniform and, for one reason or another, relatively lack- ing in variety of types and patterns of changes. For these cases, there would not be drastic differences bet- ween the results of applying methodological extremitism and methodological gradationism. To continue the anal- ogy we have previously adopted, we can again think of the structure of a house and its appearance. In a case of a simple structure with limited materials to fill out the struc- ture — such as a tent — the appearance of the house can be easily inferred from the structure and the structure is transparent under the appearance. Thus knowledge of structure and of appearance are sufficiently similar for the indiscriminating eyes to tell the differences as not to prompt us to distinguish them. What gradations there may be are very limited and there simply is not much room for steps away from the theoretical limits. The existence of these special cases lends an appearance to the ability of theories which are really about theoretical limits to explain phenomena of reality, which would be more appropriately handled by theories under methodological gradationism.

When these special cases are not being recognized for what they are, theories developed by orthodox economics seem to have made some headway in studying reality.[18] But then we should also remember that orthodox economics is also unable to break further ground beyond the small start achieved. Our bifurcation of reality and methodology and our pointing out of this special case where the respective methods yield similar results clearly explain the situation.

Constructing The Logical Map of Reality

These bifurcations of reality and methodology and their special case have thus put into proper context the role of orthodox economics with its methodological extremitism and the economics to be developed under methodological gradationism. Only the economics developed in the latter manner has the potential to satisfy the intuitive expectation that economic theories should be able, *inter alia*, to expli-cate the many salient features of the real world. The reason

---

[18] Thus, Frank Hahn claims that general equilibrium theory can make some kind of vital contribution to such issues, of certainly very great practical importance, as (a) flexible exchange rates; (b) exhaustible resources; and (c) the desirability or necessity of foreign aid. See Frank Hahn, *On the Notion of Equilibrium in Economics* (Cambridge: Cambridge University Press, 1973), p.14.

is that only such gradation with positive information about the characteristics of the qualitatively distinct less-than-perfect states (of competition, knowledge, etc.) and about the underlying mechanisms or factors responsible for them would be able to inform us about the real world. Thus, while theories about extremities are informative about the theoretical limits of an economy, it remains for theories about gradations to inform us the nature and character of the stages and the generative principles by which the economic reality moves towards or away from such extremities. The total picture would then be a logical map of possibilities about our economic reality.

That a theory has the potential to be incorporated within the boundary of such a map would then be a distinguishing mark to its ability to study the real world. This potential is, however, no guarantee for the truth of the theory which is an entirely different question. This case is similar to Popper's falsifiability criterion for scientific theory. That a theory is falsifiable only qualifies it to be possibly scientific.[19] Whether it is true depends on other conditions to be satisfied. Conversely, that a theory is unfalsifiable does not necessarily imply its invalidity, but only its disqualification from being scientific.

There is an important characteristic to this potentiality for incorporation into a logical map of possibilities. As each of the factors or mechanisms being posited is only one among possibly many others, our conception about them would have to take into account how they operate despite or because of coexisting factors. This characteristic renders each theory about a gradation a stepping stone to study further gradations and to study other factors and mechanisms within the economy related to other extremities and to factors and phenomena studied by other

---

[19] Karl R. Popper, *The Logic of Scientific Discovery* (New York: Basic Books, 1959).

disciplines. As such, theories about a gradation must at least take into account — if not give an account — of the operation of other factors and mechanisms. In other words, theories about gradation provide the interface, or at least the basis for formulating the interfacing relation between different factors and mechanisms within the same discipline as well as across different disciplines.

These stepping-stone and interfacing qualities of gradation theory provide the possibility for shaping the logical map step by step as we accumulate knowledge progressively. Thus, though we have not yet come to the problem of testing the truth of theories about gradations, we have already provided at least a partial account of how know-ledge about the economic and other social reality could progress.

The Cognitive Assumption of Orthodox Economics

One such prime example of extraction from extra-economic factors that are relevant to economics is related to man's cognitive apparatus. If the economic man is truly human, he would neither be as omnipotent as God nor as ignorant as an animal. Thus man's cognitive capacities should not be presumed to approximate too closely to either God or animal. And to specify the way in which man falls between God and animal, it is necessary to sketch the true economic man and to spell out his less-than-perfect cognitive charac-teristics.

Instead of specifying the way in which the true economic man falls between God and animal, orthodox economics has taken a short cut of making the cognitive assumption that the economic man has already achieved perfect rationality. This approach has however been forced upon it by default. Apart from the fact that the assumption of perfect rationality is needed to study theoretical limits, orthodox economics makes the assumption for several apparently justifiable reasons. First, it hopes that by cutting off economics from the study of the irrational parts of man (hence it coins the term "economic man"), economics can hopefully have a self-contained and meaningful domain of its own. Little does it know that such cutting off is not fully legitimate in that, while economics need not bother itself with the irrational parts of man, it should nevertheless be aware of the effects of such irrationalities on economic behavior.[20] Secondly, between the polarities of perfect rationality and perfect ignorance, there are no intermediate steps or theories upon which orthodox economics can relate itself to. Without a set of meaningful gradations between rationality and ignorance, it is natural that orthodox economics tends to choose the former, for nothing else could be studied on the latter unless systematic patterns of ignorance can be identified and developed in the first instance.[21] Thirdly, anxious to elevate itself to the status of physical science, orthodox economics is unwilling to claim its stake in those areas not amenable to the application of mathematical techniques, or other paraphernalia of scientific respectability as well as

---

[20] Economists who come slightly closer to this view include Kenneth E. Boulding and members of the Austrian School. Harvey Leibenstein's "Micro-micro theory," recognizing concepts like inertia, resistance to change, etc., also shows a budding awareness of such "non-optimal behavior." See Harvey Leibenstein, "Micro-Micro Theory, Agent-Agent Trade and X-Efficiency," *Economics in the Future*, Kurt Dopfer, ed. (Boulder: Westview Press, 1976). So is Lester Thurow, *op. cit.*, p.219.

[21] Thus, T.W. Hutchison argued, "Anyhow, the maximization-under-certainty postulate has proved, as a piece of simplificatory scaffolding, very difficult, or virtually impossible, to remove, while leaving standing any model or theory for which any significant degree of generality could be claimed. There is simply no general assumption to replace this oversimplified one. For there is, so to speak, only one set of correct expectations, or state of adequate knowledge, for each and every situation. But there is an endless variety of incorrect and inadequate ones, which are constantly changing, and impossible to generalise about except in arbitrary terms." See T. W. Hutchison, *op.cit.*, p.80.

those areas which appear loosely structured, if not altogether amorphous.

The concept of perfect knowledge within the orthodox framework could be further analysed into two components, namely perfect self-knowledge and perfect knowledge about the external world, in particular the market situation. The possession of perfect knowledge about the external world and the market situation is attributable either to the existence of the perfect market which transmits information instantaneously and costlessly or to the possession of complete and perfect foresight of the transactors, or both. **The combination of perfect self-knowledge, the maximizing motive and the existence of a perfect market turns the economic man into an "*economic robot,*" while the combination of perfect self-knowledge, the maximizing motive and the possession of complete and perfect foresight of the external world turns the economic man into an "*economic god.*" Whichever is the more appropriate interpretation of the orthodox doctrine, the "*true economic man*" is virtually non-existent in orthodox economics for he has implicitly been ousted by either the economic robot or the economic god.** Thus, instead of theorizing economics on the qualities of a true human being with his natural limitations, that part of orthodox economics which aims to study the real world has put itself in an impossible position, for it is in effect studying the theoretical extensions of the *economic god* or the *economic robot.* This is squarely contradicting reality, for it entails the impossibility of existence of phenomena such as remorse after choice, wisdom after the event, the effect of learning, etc.

Even the Austrian School seems caught in this dilemma. While it recognizes the seriousness of the model-reality gap generated out of the perfect rationality approach, it just manages to realize that man makes mistakes, but is unable to give an account of man's partial rationality. As a result, it has no more power than orthodox economics to study the orderly or the systematically ignorant and the irrational. It thereby has to resort to implicit assumptions that in spite of his errors, man should be able to correct these errors through learning and through the coordinating power of the market. As a result, much of its original and bright insights into the economic reality have to be compromised.[22]

Rationality and Man's Faulty Cognitive Apparatus

Almost invariably, a social science theory which purports to study human behavior or human action has to take position, in one way or another, about what would be the basic or dominant cognitive characteristics of man. It would be inconceivable for man to think or act in isolation from the characteristics of his cognitive apparatus. This is because even those parts of his actions that are seemingly guided solely by instincts are seldom devoid of cognitive content or have failed to be inspired by his sub-conscious cognition of both his external or internal realities. Indeed, man is so heavily dependent upon his cognitive apparatus and his conceptions, either handed down by tradition or developed on his own that it is difficult to reconstruct what his original instinctive endowments are.[23]

Of course, without the foundation of instincts, it would be difficult to develop his conscious values and conceptions of the world. But these instinctive endowments can provide

---

[22] For a general exposition of the Austrian School , see Israel M. Kirzner, *Competition and Entrepreneurship* (Chicago: University of Chicago Press, 1973); Ludwig M. Lachmann, *Capital, Expectations and the Market Process* (Menlo Park, California: Institute for Humane Studies, 1977); Edwin G. Dolan, ed., *The Foundations of Modern Austrian Economics* (Menlo Park, California: Institute for Humane Studies, 1976).

[23] Carl Gustav Jung, "Instinct and the Unconscious," *The Portable Jung*, Joseph Campbell, ed. (Baltimore: Penguin Books), pp. 47-59. extracted from "The Structure and Dynamics of the Psyche," Collected Works Vol.8 pars 263-282.

only a very vague direction for man to form his values and to develop his knowledge of the external world. Acting according to instinct is quick, economical in the expenditure of energy and sometimes more certain. But it is impossible to build upon strength. While acting according to conception is slower and sometimes less certain, what is lost in certainty and speed is far more than compensated for by the gain in sophistication, flexibility as well as the cumulative refinements, revisions and expansion of conceptions which enable man to build upon the legacy of his predecessors and to develop his cognitive know-how towards higher levels.

While this improvement of conceptions and cognitive know-how does lend a feeling of rationality to man, for such a capacity establishes univocably man's superiority over animals, acting according to conception is not without pitfalls and errors. In many areas, it is possible for the same patterns of errors and inadequacies to repeat themselves.[24] This is because while man's conception does help to give shape to reality, man's cognitive apparatus is not without faults or infallible. While some of these faults could be corrected by learning or through the upgrading of his cognitive know-how, the persistence of certain patterns of errors also points to the possibility that there are structural properties about his cognitive apparatus which pose limits to such corrections.

That man's cognitive apparatus and conceptions are subject to limitation is but natural. Man's conception, being his mental tools to receive and interpret experience, is basically a product of his mind.[25] Such a product, being subject to the characteristics of his concept generating mechanisms, is

---

[24] For example, in the field of perception, the perseverance of perceptual illusion has long been demonstrated by the Gestalt psychologists like W. Kohler, etc.

[25] Immanuel Kant, *Critique of Pure Reasons*, F.M. Muller tr. 2nd ed. (1896), (New York: Macmillan, 1934).

not of necessity in perfect analogue with reality.[26] Another limitation is that the adoption of many a conceptual framework often implies the exclusion of others.[27] But what is not generally realized is that beyond the narrow confines of what is commonly recognized to be rational, there exists a wide array of cognitive faults and limitations, each subject to systematic study, and each can have significant impact on man's economic actions. It is also not generally realized that part of man's cognitive instruments perform differently under varying situations and that there might be factors which can inhibit or upgrade the development of these instruments.[28] In other words, it is not fully realized that there can be meaningful and readily definable gradations between the polarity of full rationality on the one hand and the polarity of absolute ignorance on the other; gradations parts of which are subject to change over time and parts of which may remain relatively unaffected by changes in reality.

Bearing the above in mind, it would therefore be naive to assume that the cognitive make-up of man is a constant. This is simply untrue because knowledge being evolutionary, the cognitive make-up of man at different points of history are bound to differ. In particular, language, the tool on which man's conceptions critically depend on, changes. Different life situations dictate different modes of classification and new ways of articulation.[29] What parts of man's

[26] Karl R. Popper, *Conjectures and Refutations: The Growth of Scientific Knowledge* (New York: Harper and Row, 1968).

[27] Extreme cases can be seen in examples of conceptual systems such as Marxism, sociology of knowledge, etc.

[28] For example, this can be best seen in the study of the development of human consciousness by Julian Jaynes and anthropological studies in the development of the Western linear concept of time, etc. See Julian Jaynes, *The Origin of Consciousness in the Breakdown of the Bicameral Mind* (New York: Pelican Books, 1982).

[29] B. L. Whorf, *Language, Thought and Reality*, J. B. Carroll, ed.(Cambridge, Mass: The MIT Press, 1956).

cognitive characteristics are easily subject to change and what parts do not, therefore, become important questions which should have significant bearing on the study of social reality. A full-fledged cognitive science, whose domain of study encompasses different sets of gradations between the position of perfect rationality and that of absolute ignorance, thus represents the most significant foundation for all social sciences to progress further.

Unaware of the existence of such a range of faultiness of man's cognitive apparatus being amenable to systematic formulation, most social science theories have wittingly or unwittingly been making simplistic assumptions about man's cognitive make-up. They either develop along the polarity of perfect rationality to the extreme position of assuming perfect knowledge for the acting agent or formulate within the narrow confines of full ignorance or irrationality.[30] Without a backup of a full-fledged cognitive science, they are unable to stretch far beyond these polarities, which they believe to be amorphous areas that defy systematic analysis. Indeed, economic theories or any other social science theories need an intermediate or perhaps foundation science — cognitive science — for them to have access to the real world.

Introducing the Cognitive Dimension into Economics

The human situation is characterized by the limitation of knowledge. The economic man within this new framework, while not in possession of perfect knowledge, is neither in a state of absolute ignorance. He has sufficiently powerful cognitive instruments to help him to overcome part of his ignorance but at the same time he is subject to numerous constraints as a result of his cognitive limitations. His knowledge is constrained partly by his ignorance while his ignorance is partly removed by his knowledge. Through his cognitive processes, man invents new concepts to classify and to

---

[30] Behaviorism in psychology is a typical example.   *(continue in p.57)*

Part Two

Selected Themes from

The Unseen Dimensions of Wealth: Towards a Generalized Economic Theory

The Unseen Dimensions of Wealth:
Towards a Generalized
Economic Theory

by *Henry K. H. Woo*
   Hong Kong Institute of
   Economic Science
   Publication Date **October 1984**
   ISBN   **0-9613204-0-0**
   LC   **84-11910**

Approx 450 pp $35.00

Victoria Press
37782 Los Arboles Drive
Fremont, CA 94536

The Unseen Dimensions
of Wealth:
Towards a Generalized
Economic Theory

Henry K. H. Woo

*Every individual endeavors to employ his capital
so that its produce may be of greatest value ....
He generally neither intends to promote the
public interest, nor knows how much he is pro-
moting it. He intends only his own security ... only
his own gain. And he is in this led by an Invisible
Hand to promote an end which was no part of
his intention....By pursuing his own interest he
frequently promotes that of society more effectu-
ally than when he really intends to promote it.*

Adam Smith
The Wealth of Nations, 1776

The idea of the "Invisible Hand," albeit just one among
the vast store of wisdom in "The Wealth of Nations," does
epitomize the ideas and approaches to be found in this
masterpiece that established the science of economics.
While Adam Smith, the father of economics, has witnes-
sed and explicated the mechanisms behind a budding
market economy in the early stage of capitalism, subsequent unfolding of further and more complex
mechanisms propelling the growth of the capitalist economy
during the following centuries still awaits another work
comparable to scope and depth to explicate and integrate
these subsequent developments into a system of new
economic principles.

"The Unseen Dimensions of Wealth" represents a recon-
struction of economics upon a new foundation consisting
of a multitude of new conceptions — economic and
methodological — to comprehend the salient mechanisms
behind the development of the capitalist economy. To give
a foretaste of the scope, depth and originality of the
economics developed thereat, some major themes are
adapted from the book. The following contains a brief
exposition on each of these selected themes.

Theme 1 **Surplus-searching Instinct instead of Maximizing Behavior**
—Lifting Economics above Socio-cultural and Historical Constraints

Theme 2 **An Interactionist Theory of Economic Signals**
—Overcoming the Limitations of Conventional Price Theory

Theme 3 **The Economic Process as an Adaptive Process**
—Towards a Managerial Approach to Economic Performance

Theme 4 **Overhauling the Fundamental Conceptions of Economic Resources**
—Establishing the Primacy of Human Capital

Theme 5 **Towards a New Definition of Economics**
—Economics as a Development Problem instead of an Allocation Problem

Theme 6 **Establishing New First Principles in Economics**
—Incorporating Cognitive Laws and Principles into Economics

Theme 7 **Modern Capitalism as Manipulative Capitalism**
—The Cognitive Inevitability of Manipulation

Theme 8 **The Degeneration of Wealth-creating Mechanisms**
—Understanding Today's Economic Malaises in the Industrial World

Theme 9 **Transcending the Conventional Subjective -Objective Polarity**
—Admitting the "Orderly" Subjective into Economic Analysis

Theme 10 **Resolving the Market versus Planning Controversy**
—Unfolding the Myth of the Notion of the Mixed Economy

Theme 1   Surplus-searching Instinct instead of Maximizing Behavior

—*Lifting Economics above Socio-cultural and Historical Constraints*

Orthodox economics sees man as a maximizer. Within its framework, rational behavior is defined in part in terms of the maximizing behavior of the economic man. In the opinion of the Hong Kong School, this is a highly constricted assumption. This is because maximizing behavior is not the only type of rational behavior and the maximizing approach is but one of the many approaches that can be adopted in attaining man's goals. What is considered rational in one culture may not be considered so in another. Different societies possess different values that determine what ought to be pursued by their members. Even within the same culture, man need not necessarily maximize. Instead of maximizing, he may adopt the economizing approach or the compromising approach. In fact, a lot of real-life situations represent the outcome of a compromise between man's desire to maximize on the one hand and his desire to economize on the other. Pure maximizing behavior is rare.

The Hong Kong School postulates that man does not start with a structured set of wants and needs apart from the basic biological goal of lifting himself above subsistence. His other wants and needs evolve as he develops. New experiences give him insights into where his potential needs lie and lead him to formulate new goals. Maximizing behavior is normally limited to those times when man has very specific goals to pursue and when he is confident that the repertoire of his means is sufficient to help him reach these goals.

As an alternative, the Hong Kong School postulates that the rational man is guided by an instinct to search and to reap a surplus out of his efforts either in a particular situation or over a series of situations. The surplus may take the form of a tangible profit or an intangible gain in utility or satisfaction. It may also take the form of efforts economized or energy expenditure saved. This postulate is broad enough to encompass the overtly different behaviors of people in different socio-cultural systems. It allows for the possibility that the rational man can make mistakes and at times behave in a less-than-fully rational manner. It allows for the possibility that the rational man at a particular situation or for a particular period may not necessarily know where his best interest lies. It accepts the possibility for the rational man to learn, to adapt himself to problems, to restructure his priorities in response to changing circumstances and to reshuffle his goals in light of his new awareness of his needs and limitations. Methodologically, this postulate is more powerful because it makes less assumption about the ultimate nature of human motivation. It leaves enough room for other disciplines such as psychology, ethics, etc. to study the mechanisms and the contents of the surplus being searched.

Unlike the economic man who is less sure of his goals, the modern economic organisation has a much more definitive goal. In spite of this, the orthodox maximizing assumption is still too narrow. While it is safe to postulate that the economic organisation does strive to maximize its overall interest in the long run, there is no reason to assume that it should adopt the profit-maximizing approach all the time. This is indeed seldom in the modern corporation. At one time, it may prefer increasing its market share to maximizing profit. At another time, it may prefer to shift its resources to "positional goods" to protect itself against possible future loss. Sometimes, it may adopt the strategy of maximizing its corporate value instead of profit. At another time, it may compromise with other firms which may otherwise develop strident conflicts with it. Sometimes it might prefer to spend massively to build up a public image.

As in the case of the economic man, the Hong Kong School postulates that the economic organisation is incessantly in search of new approaches that, in its opinion, will maximize its long-term benefit, though it is, too, obvious that it may not be fully aware of where its best interest lies and whether the strategy it adopts will attain the objective it stipulates. It is a search process of trial and error. In a less certain condition, an organisation usually adopts more cautious strategies. Maximization as a strategy is adopted normally during periods of higher certainty, or under those market conditions where the organisation commands "positional advantages."

Adapted from
The Unseen Dimensions of Wealth
Chapter 22: Towards a New Economic
Philosophy

Theme 2   An Interactionist Theory of Economic Signals
— *Overcoming the Limitations of Conventional Price Theory*

Orthodox economics confines the study of market largely to the study of prices. By reducing economic signals to price data, orthodox economics has made economic phenomena amenable to mathematical treatment, but at the same time, it has cut itself off from the vast amount of useful knowledge that can be generated by studying non-price signals as well as by studying the signalling process.

Price data possess important signalling power because by reducing economic exchanges to a common denominator they give at least a sense of proportion, if not able to reflect precisely value or utility. Furthermore, no rational economic decision can be considered complete without having scrutinized the relevant price data. Even if the initial signal does not carry the price component, rational consideration of the opportunities embodied in a signal has to take into account related price data.

There is, however, a gross over-estimation of the signalling power of prices. The power of the market system, in the opinion of the Hong Kong School, does not lie merely in the signalling power of prices. Its power lies rather in the fact that in a decentralized market economy, a wide range of prices indicating different levels of qualities exist for most goods and services. The existence of a range of price differentials correlating quality differentials enables an economic agent to tell more precisely how prices and qualities are matched. For the consumer, such information helps him to get better value for money because he is in a position to judge more precisely what he has to pay for the quality he wants and also because he is in a position to trade between small variations in qualities and prices. As a rule, the smaller the variations he can trade between prices and qualities, the more likely he can get value for money. For the prospective investor, the presence of such subtle differentials and possibilities for marginal trade-offs between prices and qualities provide a wide-ranging data base for spotting where business opportunities can be exploited. It is these subtle price/quality differentials that provide the true signalling power of the market.

Equally important, no data including price data can have signalling power without the collaboration of a prior interpretative framework of the economic agent. For prices to function as useful signals presupposes certain background knowledge of the economic reality on the part of the economic agents. The individual economic agent's particular circumstances, values and motivations, knowledge and opinions, skills and resources, act both as the interpretative framework giving special meaning to the data that he encounters and as the screening mechanism separating them from the myriads of other data which are meaningless, superfluous or even confusing to the economic agent.

Economic signals are thus agent-specific, not reproducible and not readily transferable. The quality of an economic signal thus depends on the quality of the interpretative framework of the human agent in question. From this perspective, the absurdity of the assumption of perfect information by the orthodox doctrine becomes obvious. The fact that a set of data could only be made meaningful as a signal or a piece of valuable information to an economic agent with a specific background naturally contradicts the assumption that each and every economic agent has equal access to all types of economic signals and information in the economy.

Adapted from
The Unseen Dimensions of Wealth
Chapter 2: The Nature of Economic
Signals

**Theme 3   The Economic Process as an
Adaptive Process**
*—Towards a Managerial Approach
to Economic Performance*

Economic processes, in the opinion of the Hong Kong School, involve in varying degrees the adaptation of human agents to situations and therefore should be studied from the managerial approach. As a corollary, a central problem of economics is to study the quality and the range of adaptive activities.

Adaptation is necessary in the economic process because the knowledge and skills of the human agent, the state of his interpretative framework with which he screens opportunity signals and warning signals, the goals he sets for himself in the flux of socio-cultural norms, as well as the strategies that he adopts towards achieving such goals, are not constant factors.

Every production situation involves the application of knowledge and techniques, which are generally organized in hierarchies in the order of their degrees of abstraction. There is a core of more abstract formulae within any set of techniques, which is applicable to a wider range of situations, but beyond the core, there are peripheral formulae of different degrees of abstraction related to different prototypes of situations. If a situation is not readily classifiable into one of the prototypes, a certain degree of adaptation is required. The way of doing things in a particular situation is often a compromise between general knowledge or techniques on one hand and the specific requirements of the situation on the other.

The room for adapting general techniques by the human agent to specific situations is ample, even within the context of the organisation where standard response is generally preferred. Even if the techniques are rigidly standardized, the minute organisation or the sequencing of minor procedures may still be modified in some circumstances to suit particular situations and the personal abilities or dispositions of the human agent involved.

With respect to the quality of adaptation, the Hong Kong School distinguishes broadly two polarized states. At one end is "stereotyped adaptation." Carried to the extreme, the human agent adopting this approach tends to reduce all situations to stereotypes, and all responses to a finite set of standard programs. At the other end is "positive adaptation." At this position, the human agent takes nothing for granted. He would select the best option among different alternatives in tackling a new situation, and even in recurrent situations, he would attempt to spot any irregularities that may call for a better method of doing things. In certain economic systems, the norm is closer to that of stereotyped adaptation while in others, positive adaptation in different degrees of intensity is the rule. What constitutes the "acceptable" quality of adaptation appears to vary widely and seems to be a function of the conventions followed by a particular socio-economic system.

Since the room for adaptation by the human agent is ample, how "positively" the human agent adapts and the quality of his adaptation become central questions in the economic process. The human factor cannot simply be taken for granted. The quality of human response and adaptation can be as important, if not more so, as the amount of resources available. Within an economic organisation, an individual human agent is generally motivated to innovate and to improve upon existing techniques, provided that once he acquires a breakthrough, he will be able to reap an "innovative surplus" in recurrent situations by way of material rewards, or more leisure and comfort. How much the human agent is motivated depends in part on the extent he can retain the fruits of his innovative activities, that is, the innovative surplus that accrues to him and the extent that surplus can be converted to the most liquid form, that is, monetary reward.

Since quality is not something that can readily be enforced, coerced into existence or maintained easily by policing, the quality of adapting general techniques to specific situations is therefore governed to a significant extent by the positive attitude of the human agent, namely, the extent he is voluntarily committed to carrying a given task to its logical completion. The existence of this attitude or the lack of it, in the opinion of the Hong Kong School, can make a big difference to the overall efficiency and productivity of an economic organisation or economic system.

Adapted from
The Unseen Dimensions of Wealth
Chapter 1: The Economic Process as an
         Adaptive Process

**Theme 4   Overhauling the Fundamental
            Conceptions of Economic Resources**
            — *Establishing the Primacy of Human
            Capital*

Orthodox doctrine conceives economic resources to consist of three major factors of production, namely, labor, capital and land, which are subject to measurement and with given technology, the level of output is governed solely by the quantity of these inputs. It implicitly assumes that the market prices of these inputs can fully reflect their different qualities.

The Hong Kong School holds distinctly different views. The following gives a very brief outline of selected views of the Hong Kong School in this regard:

a)   The Hong Kong School is of the opinion that market prices alone are not capable of fully reflecting the heterogeneous qualities of inputs. The economic process being an adaptive process and the quality of adaptation being largely governed by the human factor, the same amount of physical resources within different organisational settings and market conditions tends to display different degrees of productivity which may not be fully reflected by market prices without time lags.

b)   The Hong Kong School holds the view that none of the three factors of production is technique-free and that a significant part of these factors is reducible to the techniques they embody without which they could hardly perform in the way they do. In other words, there is a more important intangible factor behind the tangible forms.

c)   The Hong Kong School also shows that all tangible forms of economic resources, be they machinery, building, land or even money capital are reducible to "human capital" in the broadest conception. The difference between what is conventionally regarded as human capital and land, machinery, money, etc. is just the form in which human capital in the broad sense is encapsulated, that is, whether human capital is encapsulated in space, in material objects, in the medium of exchange, etc. What is conventionally called human capital is just that part of what the Hong Kong School would call human capital which has not yet been encapsulated elsewhere other than in the biological organism of homo sapiens.

d) The Hong Kong School thus advances a new definition of human capital. Human capital is defined as the intangible part of human resources consisting of the following components : the techniques of doing things embodied in the individual human agent, the human capacity to adapt and to innovate, the human attitude towards the quality of work, entrepreneurship which includes the risk-taking capacity and the human capacity to mutually adapt to one another. Since economic resources are predominantly human resources and since human resources are predominantly human capital, economic resources are by and large human capital.

e) The Hong Kong School proposes that the tangible inputs of production should be more appropriately looked upon as "physical" agents of production in contrast to the intangibles which are the true "factors" of production. The former is readily quantifiable while the latter is not necessarily so. By this definition, factors of production in the conventional sense belong largely to the category of "agents of production."

Adapted from
The Unseen Dimensions of Wealth
Chapter 3: Economic Resources and
Human Capital

Theme 5   Towards a New Definition of Economics
— Economics as a Development Problem instead of an Allocation Problem

Orthodox economics acquiesces with the definition of itself as the science which studies human behavior as a relationship between ends and scarce means which have alternative uses. This "allocative" definition has unwittingly generated a grave mistake. In assuming that economic resources are necessarily scarce, it has put the allocation problem as the central problem in economics. In the perspective of the Hong Kong School, economics should not deal predominantly with the allocation problem. Before one starts to allocate, one has to explain why there is anything to allocate in the first instance. Economics, as the Hong Kong School sees it, should first explain how we have come all the way to where we are now.

It can be argued that at the micro-level, an economic agent does always face the problem of allocation. He has to allocate his time, his efforts or his other resources for the purpose of getting the most out of his apparently scarce means or limited resources. While the importance of the allocative function is undoubted, it has to be realized that this function only becomes predominant when resources are genuinely scarce. But resources are not genuinely scarce in many circumstances. Most situations where physical resources appear to be scarce turn out to be not the case. Even a moderate innovation in the techniques of doing things can often resolve these apparently scarcity situations. Even when scarcity becomes a genuine problem against certain specific ends, the human agent, if he is free to pursue his own ways, will likely develop new ways of getting round the problem. In the course of his doing so, the scarcity situation will produce its own human capital and more economic resources. Depending on the attitude and the volition of the human agent, scarcity can be a blessing in disguise.

Whether resources are scarce or abundant therefore depends critically upon the human agent himself, his goals as well as the socio-economic ethos which influence how the human agent responds to situations. Provided he is not weighed down by social or political constraints, and that he is prepared to make some present sacrifices, the human agent with definitive goals in mind is often in a position to generate new resources over time and within his own capabilities.

In the longer run the thesis of scarce resources is even less valid because the economic goals pursued by the economic agent and their priorities are not likely to remain unchanged. Unforeseen circumstances may lead to the reshuffling of existing priorities and new awareness among the economic agents may generate new goals. Predictably new goals or new priorities will generate new kinds of resources. How much resources will be generated will depend on how much emphasis or importance the human agent will attach to his new goals. Economics is thus not predominantly an allocation problem. To redeem it from this misplaced emphasis, economics must be reconstructed as a development problem, a study of how economic resources respond to changes in incentive systems and management styles in the short run and more importantly, of how economic resources grow and develop over time. Since economics is essentially a development problem, it must liberate itself from the short time frame of study to which it has subjected itself.

Adapted from
The Unseen Dimensions of Wealth
Chapter 22: Towards a New Economic
Philosophy

Theme 6   Establishing New First Principles in Economics
—*Incorporating Cognitive Laws and Principles into Economics*

To understand the complexities of economic reality, the Hong Kong School considers it fundamental to incorporate new cognitive hypotheses about the economic man. The following gives a brief outline of a few of these hypotheses:

a) **Difference in economic performance under well-structured and loosely-structured situations**

Contrary to conventional wisdom, the Hong Kong School is of the opinion that even in areas where self-interest rules, man does not always act vigilantly and intelligently to make the best use'of his cognitive instruments. In some areas, for example, in a production situation or a situation of immediate consumption, man functions within relatively well-defined boundaries where the objectives are pre-set, the constraints are clear and the role of the human agent is not equivocal. These structural elements give the situation an inner logic which is sufficiently forceful to guide the human agent to be vigilant and to make good use of his cognitive apparatus. But man as a consumer in areas of extended consumption, as an investor of effort, or as an investor of his money capital, etc. is typically facing situations which are relatively open-ended and which are too fluid to be subject to easy definition. In these circumstances where the economic man is acting as an "economic agent," as opposed to his position as a "technical agent" in the more structured situation, he tends to be relaxed, vague, and less judicious. He tends to under-utilize his cognitive apparatus and to under-invest his cognitive efforts. Hence self-interest alone without external pressure is not enough to force man to be "rational" across all situations and to apply consciously and systematically his cognitive instruments that are needed to bring about rationality of choice in open situations. This is in contra-distinction to the nature of the economic man assumed in orthodox economics.

b) **The impact of sticky human conception on economic phenomena**

Many real-world economic phenomena are not fully explicable by the orthodox framework because one important cognitive principle is being ignored, namely, man tends to hold a sticky conception of reality. A conception once formed by him tends to persist even when there is solid evidence against its empirical validity. There are a number of factors such as the compartmentalization of man's conceptual frameworks, the non-testability of many economic conceptions, the screening bias of man's interpretative framework and so on, which reinforce man's entrenchment with his original conceptions. This leads him to adopt various cognitive mechanisms to save his original framework from the assault of reality. Recognition of this hypothesis has far-reaching consequences for the understanding of economic phenomena. The growth of big firms, the development of market concentration, the vulnerability of consumers against manipulative actions of modern corporations, the entrenchment of the inflation perception, the excessively high rate of unemployment can be explained in no small part by the stickiness of man's conception and the lengthy time it takes to change over from one set of conceptions to another.

c)   **The effect of induction bias on economic actions**

Another common cognitive pitfall of man is that he tends to look at the world, in particular the future, in a linear manner. This has to do in part with his induction apparatus. Induction is a powerful tool because it enables man to make generalizations out of limited observations. But for a generalization to be validly applied, the conditions under which it is to be applied have to be equivalent in structure, if not in appearance, to those governing its initial occurrences when the generalization was first made. Failure to take this into account gives rise to the general phenomenon of "induction bias" in man's projection and prediction of the future. Induction bias is widely prevalent in man's economic actions. Coupled with his sticky conceptions, it goes a long way to explain the excess optimism and pessimism underlying every trade cycle.

> **Adapted from**
> **The Unseen Dimensions of Wealth**
> **Section 3: The Cognitive Foundation of**
> **Economic Behavior**

Theme 7   Modern Capitalism as Manipulative Capitalism
—The Cognitive Inevitability of Manipulation

The development of the modern capitalist economy is characterized by the emergence and proliferation of manipulative activities which, in the opinion of the Hong Kong School, distinguish it from previous phases of capitalism.

Manipulative activities encompass a wide range of activities that share the same characteristics, namely, the deliberate production of conditions for invisibility in the market and illusion in human perception, or in short, conditions for economic ignorance. Manipulation functions by exploiting man's cognitive weaknesses and biases. Since these weaknesses and biases are more easily exploitable under more complex situations, it is natural that manipulative activities flourish in the complex modern capitalist economy.

The proliferation of manipulative activities is brought about by the advent of the big firm and market concentration which in turn are fostered by the self-sustaining and intensifying momentum of economic growth. Out of prolonged periods of reckless growth, new factors gradually emerge which have the effect of undermining the favorable conditions for human capital formation and of inducing the formation of economically counter-productive talents. As the capitalist economy comes of age, these factors begin to gain momentum. Bit by bit they raise the threshold for entry and successful participation in the economic game. Some of these phenomena are extracted below:

a)   With decreased sensitivity due to bigness, coupled with an enlarging sheltered sector and a growing employee surplus within it, the bigger firm is not necessarily more cost-efficient than the smaller ones. To make up for these deficiencies, the bigger firm is inclined to compete through more organized exploitation of the cognitive weaknesses of the consumers.

b)   Over the market front, bigness leads the executives of these organisations to think in terms of market share and a longer range future. Naturally, the data circulating in the market at any one time plus data frozen in past records are highly inadequate to provide a reasonably complete basis for decisions of such scale. Accordingly, investment commitments have to depend heavily upon certain "rationalistic parameters" such as demographic characteristics, statistical projections of cost trends, broad indicators of future demand for products of a certain broad category. The quality of these exercises depends very much upon the quality of the interpretative frameworks of the decision-makers. Even with the best interpretative frameworks available, the margin of error of necessity increases as these investment decisions extend into a longer-range future. To make up for the margin of error thus generated, big organisations have no choice but to rely on the manipulation of the market, adopting methods such as massive advertising, controlling of retail outlets, lobbying for more favorable government regulations, etc.

c)   Modern technology gives rise to a wide array of products whose sophistication necessitates vast experimental and developmental work before commercialization is possible. Since it is highly difficult for any management to predict the pattern of consumer preferences years ahead, consumers have to be manipulated to accept the products when they are launched in the market.

Manipulation has become the central strategy behind the economic actions of big organisations. The bigger they become, the more they have to depend on manipulation for their survival and their continuing to grow big. The manipulative approach proves very successful particularly in the earlier phases of adopting such an approach. This success is well-founded from the cognitive viewpoint. The economic agent's cognitive traits make him susceptible to manipulation. His inclination to imitate subjects him easily to manipulative actions. Also the nature of society's mass information dissemination process naturally exposes him to easy manipulation.

The advent of manipulation gives the bigger firm a competitive edge over the smaller ones. Of particular importance, economies of scale exist in manipulative activities. Only those firms that can afford and are persistent over long periods can win in this game in the long run.

Adapted from
The Unseen Dimensions of Wealth
Chapter 12: Growth and the Advent of
Manipulation

Theme 8   The Degeneration of Wealth-creating Mechanisms
— *Understanding Today's Economic Malaises in the Industrial World*

With the advent of bigness and market concentration, the signalling power of the data in circulation in the market, in particular the price data, is much reduced. Prices come to be determined by what the big corporations think the consumers can absorb under their manipulative power. When more prices come to be "administered," outsiders are cut off from the signalling functions of prices on value, cost, production efficiency or opportunities. The need for the big corporation to "administer" prices is attributable to the practical difficulty of ascertaining precisely the manipulative cost that has to be incurred as well as the higher risk involved in the marketing of products or services which depends heavily on manipulative techniques. Invariably this leads to higher markups. By corollary, the proliferation of these activities leads to the raising of the threshold for entry and for successful participation by new entrants.

With prospective entrants discouraged and consumers subject to easy exploitation, corporations that hold command positions or manipulative power over the market reap handsome surpluses. Manipulation yields increasing returns to scale. So do command positions. Over time, the profits acquired by these corporations become dissociated from their efficiency, their ability to compete on price terms, their ability to spot true market opportunities or to nurture innovative abilities. Over time, their profits are related more to their ability to manipulate, to create consumer illusion, to corner the market, to circumvent and exploit government regulations as well as their performance in the newly emerging "wealth transfer game." In time, these corporations are no longer competing with one another within the narrow margins of cost competition. Breakthroughs in cost reduction methods are over-shadowed by new manipulative ideas which can sway the preferences of consumers, or by manipulative techniques that succeed in exploiting or circumventing loopholes in regulations.

Within the corporation itself, as its sheltered sector grows, the internal manipulation among its members against one another intensifies. To expand or to protect his existing surplus, an employee needs to magnify the overt significance of his job and to belittle the importance of other people holding competing positions. He has to make it more difficult for his competitors to perform effectively and to hold back important data from being circulated outside his sphere of influence.

These manipulative actions are disincentives to human capital formation. They render the acquisition of productive techniques and knowledge less desirable than the acquisition of manipulative techniques. They reduce the inclination to innovate at the grassroots level. Another aspect of human capital, namely the human agent's responsibility towards the quality of work and towards the completion of a job also suffers, for within the sheltered sector, performances are difficult to assess as the market fails to play the vigilant role of a watchdog against the incompetent. Naturally too, another aspect of human capital, namely, the collaboration between human agents suffers as each manipulator conspires to undermine the performance of another. Useful data deliberately held back from general circulation reduce the chances for opportunity signals to emerge and inhibit important warning signals from being transmitted across the organisation.

Over time, growing manipulative and positional profits produce corporate giants. The economic world is no more what it was once envisaged by the earlier classical economists. Within these corporate giants, the concern of the top management graduallly drifts away from perfecting existing techniques of production, innovating new technologies and even developing new marketing ideas. The scramble for rapid results and overt performances favor manipulative activities like takeovers, acquisitions and mergers, events that have virtually nothing to do with real production or productivity. Increasingly the game of wealth transfer begins to overshadow the concern for real production. These activities tend to be destructive to human capital formation and render the existing stock of productive human capital ineffective by injecting artificial and alien elements into it.

Manipulation is a negative sum game in the long run for the economy as a whole. It increases the internal friction and reduces the efficiency of an economic system and adds to the cost of its output. As manipulative activities intensify, the consumer has to pay a higher manipulative "premium." Manipulation being a negative sum game, there is theoretically no limit as to how far this manipulative overhead on the economy as a whole will grow, and in so far as its growth is unchecked, wealth is being sucked into this vast and bottomless "blackhole."

Adapted from
The Unseen Dimensions of Wealth
Chapter 13: Consequences of Manipulation

Theme 9   Transcending the Conventional Subjective - Objective Polarity

— Admitting the "Orderly" Subjective into Economic Analysis

The methodology adopted by the Hong Kong School is founded upon a conception of subjectivity in contra-distinction to the common conception, which associates the subjective with the fanciful, whimsical, arbitrary, biased, etc. The theory of subjectivity adopted by the Hong Kong School is that systematic enquiry about the subjective is both possible and necessary. There are structural features internal to the human situation that are orderly and thereby capable of being the subject of systematic enquiry. The problem is to identify and to extract them.

Many factors converge to foster a lot of features common to the organising principles, internal orders and structures across diverse individuals. Common biological endowments and instincts, common ecological niche requiring certain skills and attitude in order to survive, common cognitive instruments, common structures in the languages used, the capacity of learning by imitation, the dependence on cultural transmission, the propensity to emulate the leader, social pressure towards conformity, the economy of mental effort in adopting common practices instead of thinking out one's own way of doing things, etc., all converge so that the internal orders and structures of individuals within or across different cultures are qualitatively similar. These internal orders and structures share an important characteristic with what is commonly regarded as a key feature of objectivity. That is, they are not amenable to the wishes, the whims, the conveniences and the contingent requirements of the moment of the individual, etc. But they are not objective in the conventional sense of being directly open to inter-subjective testing as in the case of there being such and such a physical object in such and such a location at such and such a time.

The fundamental reason why the Hong Kong School emphasizes the need to probe into the "orderly" part of the subjective is that what is ordinarily considered objective, that is, the observables, the tangibles, the measurables are generally far from being adequate for the understanding of the human and social reality or for predictive purposes. What is observable commands usually too small a base for theorizing. What is measurable represents in many instances the aggregate outcome of divergent situations or conflicting under-currents and what is tangible often conceals highly subjective elements behind it. They have no exclusive claim to the totality of objective existents. Most importantly, the observable and measurable are largely *expost* material, i.e. they represent the "outcome" of the "orderly" part of the subjective factors at work and therefore may come too late in the causal sequence to serve as the basis for predictive purposes.

The role assigned to the "objective" in a social science theory in the methodology of the Hong Kong School is therefore very different from what is conceived in the conventional sense and in mainstream economics. From the former viewpoint, the failure to recognize and to take into account this "broadened" conception of the objective has serious repercussions for theorization in economics. Mal-treating the "orderly" subjective may lead to the abandonment of what is "truly" objective. It may lead to the building of theories which overload their bases, and as a result, sever their links with reality. It fact, many inadequacies in the development of economic theorizing arise from a lack of understanding of the above methodology. The contrast between mainstream economics and the theories developed under such a methodology, in short, is that the former does not question the conventional boundaries of the objective and tailor economic theories to suit the "objective," whereas the latter extends the realm of the "objective" to serve the needs of economic theorizing.

Adapted from
The Unseen Dimensions of Wealth
Chapter 22: Towards a New Economic
Philosophy

Theme 10 Resolving the Market versus Planning Controversy
—Unfolding the Myth of the Notion of the Mixed Economy

In the economic process of a decentralized economy, market data serve three different functions. At the initial stage of an economic action or decision, market data might "catch the eye," so to speak, of the economic agent and stimulate him to transform the data into signals via his interpretative framework. At a later stage, market data can be more systematically searched to check or elaborate upon an initial idea or to rationalize it into an economic decision. Finally, market data serve to assess the results of an economic action. Market data, however, are not the only parameters involved in an economic decision. Rationalistic parameters representing largely aggregate data frozen in past records such as income per capita, demographic trends, etc. also play a useful albeit supplementary role of closing the gap left by the inadequacies in market data.

In a highly decentralized market where the individual tends to take market data as a given, the limits of market data can act as a natural constraint to his economic decisions or actions. This position is fundamentally altered with the advent of bigness. Chief executives of the big firm wittingly or unwittingly make investment commitments to tap "opportunities" far beyond what the existing market data can be stretched to indicate. To fill the gap left out by market data, the big corporation has to rely increasingly on rationalistic parameters and its manipulative power over the market.

The heavy reliance on rationalistic parameters makes the big corporations in industrial nations look like they are acquiring some of the characteristics of the planning bureaucrats of the socialist countries. But beyond the superficial similarity between big corporations in the Western world and the economic units in the socialist countries, there are diametrically opposite characteristics. For example, the Western corporations can only manipulate by subtle persuasion whereas the socialist planning authority can manipulate by threats of force and by sheer exercise of political power. The big corporation in the West, while able to ignore the market in the short run, has to be aware of the manipulative limits of the market and subscribe to the verdict of the market in the long run. On the other hand, the planning authority can persistently and even in the long run ignore market signals. Differences also lie in the criteria adopted in their rationalistic planning. The socialist economic organisations have to get their plans rationalized by many extra-economic criteria.

With this awareness, new and general criteria emerge which can be used to assess the appropriateness of both market decisions that have significant planning content and economic plans that may enlist the help of market data, as well as their respective qualities. At the micro-level, these questions include some of the following: in a planning decision, how much can the functions of the market be brought in and whether or how far the roles of these market functions can be increased? Can subsequent market reality be more prominently and profitably recognized in assessing the manipulative limits of the market? What margin of error can a plan tolerate before it fails? When the market reality or the market manipulation limits are different from the plan, what types of adjustment mechanisms can be built into the plan to take into account such differences? On a macroscopic level, some of the questions to ask are: what kind of planning decisions are liable to command higher wealth-creating effects? What are the conditions necessary for economic plans to realize their wealth-creating potential? What types of planning decisions have wealth-destroying effects and what conditions would induce such effects to work? How can the latter conditions be removed or such negative effects be alleviated? What types of rationalistic parameters are liable to produce wider margin of error and how can the gap be narrowed?

The decision to plan or not to plan, from the viewpoint of the Hong Kong School, need not merely be an ideological one, for answers to the questions posed in the above represent new criteria that can be applied to assess planning decisions and market decisions with significant planning content. With the help of these new criteria, a more articulate framework of analysis of the planning content of a market decision, we are also in a better position to see the irrelevance of the idea of the mixed economy. The long standing controversy over the superiority of the market versus planning has to be recognized as incapable of further progress unless it is reformulated in terms of these new criteria that must be developed.

Adapted from
The Unseen Dimensions of Wealth
Chapter 22: Towards a New Economic
Philosophy

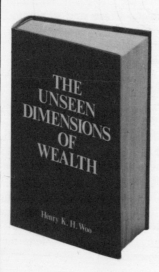

articulate unforeseen situations, thus breaking down
what originally are constraints on him. But no matter
how much effort he makes, the fact remains that he is
incapable of knowing even to a moderate extent the
vast breadth of the unknown and the uncertainties that
lie around and ahead of him. What is at issue is not
whether he is ignorant or not, but the extent of his
ignorance;[31] how he responds to it and whether or not
and how far his responses can be improved.To understand the implication of all these on man's economic
behavior, the Hong Kong School considers it paramount
to study the cognitive characteristics of the economic
man, to introduce into the fundamental framework of
economics a new set of abstractions about the underlying invariants governing man's capacity for knowledge,
his cognitive strengths and weaknesses, biases and
constraints and thereby to develop a new perspective
for critical diagnosis of and synthesis with existing
economic categories. The true economic man must
return, so to say, from his exile.

We need to further point out that, with respect to man's
mental products in general, economic theory should not
on the one hand presume man to be so mechanical and
uncreative as not capable of developing new or even
revolutionary insights but, on the other hand, economics
must capture for its foundation some invariants about
man's cognitive apparatus to build upon. This is because,
on the one hand, man's economic action is dependent
upon the use of his cognitive apparatus. So any theory in
economics which fails to take this into account would be
inadequate in some way. On the other hand, some
invariants about man's cognitive apparatus must be captured. Otherwise we would be implying that with every
major advance in man's intellectual and creative achieve-

---

[31] Thus, George J. Stigler says, "And, just as analysis of man's shelter and
apparel would be somewhat incomplete if cold weather is ignored, so also
our understanding of economic life will be incomplete if we do not systematically take account of the cold winds of ignorance." See "The Economics of
Information," *Journal of Political Economy*, LXIX (1961), 213-15.

ment, a new economics must be written, which is clearly absurd. When one looks at the features about man's cognitive apparatus which economics has to extract and abstract for its foundation, and when one looks at the content of man's major advances in ideas and creativity, one can see that there is nothing paradoxical about there being invariants about man's cognitive apparatus and that the intellectual and creative achievements of man can be marvellous and unpredictable.

What economics needs to be concerned about are the structural strengths and weaknesses of man's cognitive apparatus rather than the content of the product of man's intellect and creativity. For example, one such invariant is the universal cognitive weakness of misplaced concreteness. While man's intellectual achievements have brought the frontier of our academic knowledge to great depths of abstraction, misplaced concreteness as a general phenomenon among the typical economic agent still persists.

Both in man's phylogenetic and ontogenetic development, it is specific incidents and concrete objects that claim his immediate attention.[32] It is no wonder that the development of his cognitive apparatus should produce conceptions that are geared to the concrete. It is also true that man seldom stays on the level of the concrete very consistently. On the one hand, he uses analogy to generalize the concrete cases.[33] On the other hand, his internal subjective expectations and demands on the external world have to be put in general terms. These, however, are just seeming exceptions to our general assertion that man's cognitive apparatus is biased towards the concrete. Generalization by analogy is unsystematic and often self-contradictory. Internal demands

---

[32] There is a parallel in man's study of language. For example, even a philosopher of Ludwig Wittgenstein's calibre began studying language in terms of concepts about physical particulars to the neglect of grammatical structure (as studied by Noam Chomsky).

[33] Thus, historically the first formulations of human wisdom have always been in the form of parables and allegories such as the teachings of the Bible, Greek and other mythologies, etc.

often generate normative conceptions only. They still leave man's cognitive apparatus rather weak in relation to the general and universal behind the concrete incidents of the objective external world. Thus, this is one reason for misplaced concreteness. Another reason is that conceptions being the internally originated products of our mind, there is no reason why our first attempt, or even the first few attempts, to conceptualize the world must be appropriate. As we usually start with the concrete, our cognitive errors are thereby mostly in the direction of misplaced concreteness.

An aspect of man's intellectual achievement is his effort to get out of the above limitation. But in spite of such efforts, misplaced concreteness being a structural property about the development of cognitive apparatus, still remains. It is an invariant not affected by man's intellectual and creative advances. Man's greatest ideas and inventions are achieved in spite of, or sometimes even prompted by, misplaced concreteness and other starting weaknesses and strengths of our cognitive apparatus. They do not obliterate the existence of such structural weaknesses and strengths.

We can similarly argue for other characteristics of the cognitive apparatus which the science of economics has to extract and abstract for its foundation. **With the above distinction between achievements in intellectual and creative products on the one hand, and structural properties of the cognitive apparatus on the other, we can see why it is possible for a cognitively - based economics to explain both economic achievements in terms of advances in ideas and economic problems in terms of the invariants of his cognitive apparatus.**

Appendix One

A Hong-Kong-Inspired Theory

*"Hong Kong is a shining star — an example of an
underdeveloped territory that has achieved spec-
tacular economic success with no resources other
than the talents and hard work of its
people......Hong Kong is an extraordinary city full
of vitality. It has our great admiration."*

**George Shultz
Secretary of State, U.S.A.
On his visit to Hong Kong
1984**

The background to the new paradigm introduced in the
preceding section is Hong Kong, a land of unique
economic success in the past three decades. But this

paradigm, while nurtured and inspired by the Hong Kong situation, is far from being restricted to the Hong Kong economic reality. It is a self-contained body of economic knowledge and methodology capable of explaining economic phenomena across historical periods, geographical boundaries and cultural backgrounds.

But this new paradigm does, to some considerable extent, reflect observations and real-life cases drawn from the Hong Kong economic experience. This is inevitable, for no academic paradigm can be free from the peculiarities of its time, the socio-economic ethos of its breeding ground and the particular problems faced by its thinkers. To understand more fully the nature of this paradigm, it is useful to examine how it is related to the Hong Kong background. For those who are not too familiar with the economic background of Hong Kong, it is perhaps helpful to have an introduction to the economic position of Hong Kong in the global context.

Hong Kong is a city with a population of 5.5 million, occupying an area of 400 sq. miles at the tip of South China. Among other things, it is
- the world's largest exporter of garments, toys and games;
- the world's major supplier of light consumer items including clocks and watches, plastic and artificial flowers, batteries, watchbands, candles, electric fans, etc;
- the second busiest container port in throughput in the world after Rotterdam;
- the second largest shipowning center in the world;
- the third largest international banking and financial center in the world;
- the third largest diamond trading market in the world;
- the third largest international gold market.

On top of the above, Hong Kong has

- a GNP per capita only lower than that of Japan in Asia;
- the second highest per capita consumption of electricity in Asia;
- on a per capita basis, more bank branches or representative offices than any other territory in the world;
- the highest telephone density in South-East Asia;
- the highest vehicle density in the world next to Monaco.

Many factors have contributed towards Hong Kong's economic miracle. Among others, the often quoted ones are Hong Kong's economic policy of free enterprise, its free port status, its excellent infrastructure, its low rates of taxation, the availability of a skilled, industrious and highly disciplined work force and the adaptability of its entrepreneurs.

But this taxonomic account is far from being adequate to penetrate into the generative mechanisms which make Hong Kong tick. It is insufficient for us to grasp, so to speak, the "spirit" of the place; for all the above remarkable achievements were made with virtually no physical resources, with only meagre starting capital, with a population mostly lacking formal education in its initial stage of economic development, with a myopic colonial government without any intent of elevating the place to a world economic power and within a state of uncertainty about its political future.

Not only is this kind of taxonomic account far from being adequate, but there is also no theory we can borrow from orthodox economics that is capable of explaining such exceptional performance and of confronting the phenomena of Hong Kong to the full. This discrepancy between orthodox theory and the Hong Kong reality naturally stimulates us towards enquiring into the causes of the discrepancy and, as a consequence, towards constructing a more general theory that can encompass the Hong Kong position. While the logical link between the economic success of Hong Kong and the economics advocated by us is far less straight forward than that of an example and its generalization, the phenomena of Hong Kong do provide the intellectual inspiration for developing this new economics.

As can be expected, a small place with such breathtaking achievements must be displaying a high level of economic activities and intensive utilization of economic resources. In Hong Kong, the same factory premise and equipment are being used for more hours a day than many other places in the world. In rush times, many factories work night shifts for days on end. The same people who work in one factory in the day may go to work in another in the evening. While women are legally not allowed to work overtime beyond a certain limit, law-breaking is common. In Hong Kong few businessmen are content to have a single line of business. Most of them engage themselves in more than one type of business and the money capital generated in one business is not infrequently shifted temporarily for use in another business. In other words, the economic resources in Hong Kong have an incredibly higher rate of turnover than the same amount of resources would have done in other parts of the world. Indeed, the production system of Hong Kong does not end with the cottage factories nor with the small workshops in the back street. Involved daily in the production processes are not only full-time workers, casual workers but also in varying degrees, housewives, old folks and children in their homes, assembling parts of plastic toys, making embroideries and beads, trimming thread ends off ready-to-wear garments. In months of boom, especially nearing the year-end, the whole of Hong Kong is turned in effect into one big production factory rushing shipments to beat deadlines.

In other words, we can witness not only an intensive rate of utilization of resources in Hong Kong, but more important, we cannot fail to be impressed by the full prepared-

ness of its human agents regardless of their levels of education to spot, to grasp and to exploit opportunities, to enter
new ventures regardless of their initial endowments and
sometimes the risks involved, to re-enter the economic
game failure after failure regardless of how much or how
little they have learned from the earlier experiences. We
also cannot fail to be impressed by the intensive communi-
cation between the human agents in Hong Kong, by their
close and frequent contacts, a phenomenon made possible
by the excellent yet low-cost infrastructure of Hong Kong,
which in turn is made possible by geographical compact-
ness of the place.

In short we are witnessing a kind of "grassroots capitalism"
flourishing at its peak in Hong Kong. Awe and wonder
apart, we cannot help appreciating the power of *the human
factor in action*, how much man can do with meagre
resources, how much man can create through his volition,
how elastic or adaptive man can be under the lure of a
better tomorrow. These achievements of Hong Kong thus
spark us to a deep reflection on the importance of the
adaptive capability, the role of the link between reward
and effort, the part played by the human aspiration, the
significance of the human pursuit towards spotting and
exploiting the opportunity signal, and in a nutshell, *the role
of the human factor in the equation of economic process
and economic development.* The "spirit" of the place, so
to speak, is manifested in the liveliness, dynamism and the
vitality of its human agents in their endless and untiring
pursuit of opportunities.

Unavoidably, this human factor enters our paradigm in
many significant ways. The admission or more properly,
the re-admission of the human factor into formal economic
discourse of necessity brings with it related "subjective"
concepts. But these subjective concepts are not the "ordinarily" subjective in the sense of being the unobservable,
the undefinable, or even the whimsical. They are the "orderly" subjective concepts which are subject to systematic
formulation and scientific refutation. Furthermore, the con-

cepts that we introduce, such as reward-effort link, human capital, adaptation, economic signal, etc. are not merely economic concepts possessing both the subjective and objective dimensions, but they also possess substantial cognitive contents as well. And it is the breadth and openness of such concepts and their consistency with the human reality that enable them to transcend the Hong Kong situation and to become applicable across historical periods, geographical boundaries and cultural backgrounds.

Appendix Two

A Comparison between Conventional Economics and the Hong Kong School

A. Basic Assumptions	Conventional Economics	Hong Kong School
Cognitive assumption	perfect rationality,perfect knowledge or foresight	man possesses a powerful yet faulty cognitive apparatus, the structural strengths and weaknesses of which are subject to systematic study and have important bearing upon economic behaviors and actions
Behavioral assumption	utility or profit maximization	surplus-searching instinct responding to opportunity signals; maximization largely restricted to situations with clear goals and known effectiveness of the means employed
Economic-setting	a decentralized market economy with perfect information and perfect competition	no restricted assumption
Definition of rationality	the calculating, infallible man maximizing utility	various gradations of rationality and irrationality exist; the economic man can be, at times or even repeatedly, irrational where he is subject to the faultiness of his cognitive apparatus

Basic concern of the discipline	economics is an allocation problem; allocative efficiency as yardstick of economic performance	economics is a growth problem; the study of the emergence and operation of wealth-creating mechanisms and processes
Economic resources	tangible, measurable, perfectly divisible and substitutable	consists chiefly of human resources and intangibles; most types of capital represent human capital encapsulated in different forms; factors of production should be distinguished from agents of production
Economic processes	processes which lead to or away from states of equilibrium;	economic processes are adaptive processes, involving essentially the application of the cognitive know-how of an economic agent to specific situations; no need to be related to states of equilibrium or disequilibrium
Time	ahistorical	can be both historical and ahistorical
Scope of study	applicable essentially to large, decentralized economies	applicable to economies of all sizes

B.	Conventional Economics	Hong Kong School
Methodology		
Basic method employed	"Methodological Extremitism" — extremity conditions used as initial assumptions in order to study the theoretical limits of the decentralized economic system, in particular the allocative efficiency	"Methodological Gradationism" — a theory should allow meaningful gradations to be discovered between polarities in order to be able to formulate reality
Key concepts	strictly economic concepts	some concepts ought to have both economic and cognitive contents
Interface with other Disciplines	interfacing not allowed for	self-sufficient but open system so that interfacing with concepts from other disciplines is possible, in particular with concepts from cognitive science
Demarcation between the subjective and the objective	objective existents are confined to the measurable, the observable or the tangible; essentially a reductionist approach	objective existents broadened to encompass the "orderly subjective"
The Nature of Refutation	quantitative/mathematical; refutation underdeveloped and often mis-applied	chiefly qualitative supplemented by quantitative refutation
Distinction between "real" factors and "nominal" factors	money, credit as nominal factors	no distinction ought to be made; all factors have to operate via man's interpretative framework and are therefore "real".

C. **Micro-economics**	**Conventional Economics**	**Hong Kong School**
Scope	equated largely to price theory, to phenomena that have a price measurement	prices are only a part of the micro-economic phenomena, non-price data such as quality differences, price/quality differentials, rationalistic parameters are almost as important
Perfect competition	a plausible assumption	cognitively false for theoretical discourse
Equilibrium	equilibrating forces exist which can bring an economy back to some "natural" order	equilibrium is the resultant of certain cognitive factors at work, of convergent patterns of man's imitative behaviors; economics should emphasize on economic processes rather than on the states of equilibrium
Economic signals	equated to market prices	any data screened by an economic agent indicating the existence of exploitable opportunities; economic signals are agent-specific
Clearing of market	all markets can be cleared in principle via the price adjustments	markets tend to clear but there is no guarantee; uncleared markets exist
Theory of production	essentially mechanistic; technology and other things being equal, level of output is determined solely by the quantities of inputs	essentially managerial with substantial room for human adaptation; the level and quality of output may be closely or loosely related to the quantity of inputs
Market versus planning	sharp distinction, representing two polarized economic systems	rationalistic parameters have a role to play in many market decisions; the evaluation of market and planning decisions should be subject to a set of more subtle criteria
significance of micro-economic theory	only part of economics, to be supplemented by macro-economic theories	economic theory is essentially micro-economic theory; "methodological individualism"

D.	Conventional Economics	Hong Kong School
Macro-economics		
Validity of theory	valid macro-economic theories exist	macro-economic theories, where they were valid, are merely micro-tautologous
Macro-economic aggregates	basic building blocks of macro-economic theory	serves useful signalling function for monitoring the state of affairs within the economy and checking function for the study of micro-economics
Macro-economic correlations	supposed to yield macro-economic laws upon extensive search and analysis	provide useful checking function for micro-economics; incapable of yielding macro-economics laws that are not micro-tautologous
Macro-economic theories	legitimate theories that should be a separate branch of economic study; need to rest on a sound micro-economic foundation	economic theories are basically micro-economic in nature; "methodological individualism" holds
Terminology	—	to avoid confusion, conventional conception of macro-economics should be split into two parts, a) aggregate economics to encompass the study of macro-economic aggregates and correlations b) macro-economic or social-wide phenomena which are the outcome of micro-economic forces at work

We welcome questions and comments on our views. Please write to our Hong Kong head office or our U.S. correspondence address.

HONG KONG INSTITUTE OF ECONOMIC SCIENCE

Head Office: 48, Hillwood Road, Suite 1304, Kowloon, Hong Kong
Tel: 3-7238841 Telex: 57201 RANDM HX

U.S. Correspondence: 37782 Los Arboles Drive, Fremont, CA 94536
Tel: 415-793-1069